Survey of Credit Underwriting Practices

2007

Office of the Comptroller of the Currency

October 2007

Contents

Survey of Credit Underwriting Practices: 2007

Introduction

The Office of the Comptroller of the Currency (OCC) earlier this year conducted its 13th annual survey of credit underwriting practices. The survey identified trends in lending standards and credit risk over the past 12 months for the most common types of commercial and retail credit offered by national banks.

The 2007 survey included the 78 largest national banks by asset size and covered the 12-month period ending March 31, 2007. Although mergers and acquisitions have altered the survey population, it has covered substantially the same group of banks for the past 10 years. All companies in the 2007 survey had total assets in excess of $2 billion and their aggregate total loan portfolio as of year-end 2006 was approximately $3.2 trillion, which represented over 85 percent of all outstanding loans in the national banking system. Large banks referenced in the subsequent comments are the 20 largest banks by asset size that are supervised in the OCC's Large Bank Supervision department; the other banks are supervised in the OCC's Mid-Size/Community Bank Supervision (M/CBS) department.

Examiners-in-charge of the surveyed banks were asked a series of questions concerning overall credit trends for 18 commercial and retail credit products. The survey also included, for the first time, an assessment of underwriting standards for credit exposures related to hedge funds. This information will be analyzed and will be included in future surveys as trends develop or information warrants. For purposes of this survey, commercial credit was grouped into 12 categories: agricultural, asset-based lending, commercial construction, residential construction, other commercial real estate, commercial leasing, international, large corporate, leveraged, middle market, small business, and hedge funds. Retail products included seven categories: affordable housing, credit cards, indirect consumer paper, conventional home equity, high loan-to-value (LTV) home equity, other direct consumer, and residential first mortgages.

The term "underwriting standards," as used in this report, refers to the conditions under which credit is extended, such as collateral, loan maturities, pricing, and covenants, that banks establish when originating or renewing loans. Conclusions about "easing" or "tightening" are drawn from OCC examiners' observations over the prior 12 months. A conclusion that the underwriting standards for a particular loan category have eased or tightened does not necessarily indicate that all the standards for that particular category have been adjusted. Rather, it suggests that the adjustments that did occur had the net effect of easing or tightening the aggregate conditions under which credit was extended.

Part I of this report summarizes the overall results of the survey. Part II depicts the survey results in graphs and tables.

Part I—Overall Results

Primary Findings

- Commercial and retail credit underwriting standards eased for a fourth consecutive year.
- The 2007 survey reflected a divergence of commercial underwriting standards by institution size. Large banks continued to ease standards, especially for leveraged and large corporate products. Mid-size banks eased standards modestly, while community banks tightened standards.
- More banks eased retail underwriting standards than tightened, primarily due to competition. Easing was concentrated in the large bank group.

Commentary on Credit Risk

Commercial credit performance metrics such as level of nonperforming and adversely risk-rated loans remain very healthy, although examiners have noted slight deterioration in recent months. Examiners continue to report weakening of loan structures, including minimal amortization requirements and less frequent financial maintenance covenants, for large corporate and leveraged loans. Loan structures that require little to no amortization and lack meaningful covenants to monitor borrower performance increase credit risk for both credit originators and investors. Weaker loan structures may mask performance deterioration and defer problem loan recognition.

Because originating/syndicating banks have limited appetite for retaining large corporate credits on their own balance sheets under the terms that existed in 2006 and early 2007, they typically have followed an "originate-to-distribute" model, earning fees from loan originations while transferring the credit risk to institutional investors. For the past several years, originating banks have underwritten larger merger/acquisition, buyout, and recapitalization transactions with increasingly accommodative terms to satisfy strong institutional investor demand for credit assets. The availability of easy credit terms and abundant institutional liquidity have fueled corporate restructuring activity. Credit spreads, or the compensation for taking credit risk, narrowed to levels that, when combined with weaker credit terms and more aggressive borrower leverage, indicate credit risk was mispriced.

Institutional investors have drawn comfort from strong corporate earnings and cash flow, and therefore have been willing to accept more accommodative repayment terms and higher borrower leverage. In some transactions, for example, borrowers have the option to make cash interest payments or simply to capitalize them. These deferred and/or negatively amortizing structures make it more likely that investors will have to rely upon refinancing as a source of repayment for many leveraged loan transactions. Analysis of the borrower's ability to repay, a fundamental principle of credit, diminished in importance given investors' demand for product and higher yielding investments.

The OCC again notes the potential credit, liquidity, and reputation risks for national banks that originate and sell syndicated credits. National banks that use an originate-to-distribute business model should ensure underwriting standards are consistent with safe and sound banking practice and are not unduly compromised by anxiety for fee income during periods of excessive market liquidity.

Over the past several months, and subsequent to examiner responses on the OCC's underwriting survey, financial market liquidity has eroded due to concerns about the potential implications of weakness in subprime mortgage assets and the large pipeline of pending leveraged loan originations. Institutional investors have begun to demand more traditional credit protections, lower borrower leverage, and higher compensation for taking credit risk. These underwriting changes are an expected and healthy response to the liquidity-driven excesses of the past few years. The OCC expects that both credit originators and investors will refocus on fundamental credit principles, most particularly analyzing a borrower's capacity to repay. The OCC also expects that national banks will underwrite credit exposures with a more balanced perspective on risk and return over the full range of liquidity conditions.

Although asset quality performance of retail portfolios remained satisfactory, delinquency levels increased slightly while losses remained stable. Overall, more banks eased underwriting standards for retail credit than tightened, primarily due to competition. Retail credit standards were unchanged in two-thirds of the surveyed banks. Reduced documentation requirements and relaxed underwriting criteria, coupled with the increasing level of consumer debt and potential slowdown of the economy, could magnify retail risk levels.

There have been significant changes in market conditions and product performance since the survey was completed, especially as they relate to residential mortgage and home equity lending. As a result, many national banks have tightened underwriting standards for various residential real estate products and channels or discontinued some products all together.

Commercial Underwriting Standards

In 2007, banks continued a four-year trend of easing commercial underwriting standards. Examiners cited robust competition and product/portfolio performance as the primary reasons for easing commercial credit underwriting standards. Twenty banks reported easing commercial standards in 2007, primarily in the large bank group; 13 of the 20 reported easing for a third consecutive year.

	All Banks—Commercial Products			
	2004	2005	2006	2007
Eased	13%	34%	31%	26%
Unchanged	75%	54%	63%	58%
Tightened	12%	12%	6%	16%

Continued easing in overall underwriting standards, combined with commercial real estate concentrations in community and mid-size bank portfolios, underscores examiners' assessments that commercial credit risk is increasing.

Examiners anticipate that this change in underwriting, combined with the currently uncertain economic environment, will further increase commercial credit risk over the next 12 months for 58 percent of the sampled banks in several products: leveraged lending, commercial real estate lending, large corporate, and middle market loans.

Product Trends

Trends in product underwriting reflect continued material easing in leveraged and large corporate lending, which generates significant fee income for those who originate and distribute the credits. Examiners did not report any banks tightening underwriting standards in these two products in the 2007 survey, and only one bank tightened standards in either product during the past three years combined. Of additional concern is increased reporting in the survey that some institutions have not altered their existing written underwriting guidance or policies, but in practice have compromised their underwriting standards to increase asset volumes and income.

	Large Corporate Loans			
	2004	2005	2006	2007
Eased	17%	32%	49%	40%
Unchanged	67%	68%	51%	60%

	Leveraged Loans			
	2004	2005	2006	2007
Eased	15%	32%	61%	67%
Unchanged	85%	68%	31%	33%

Examiners indicate that leveraged lending credits have become more aggressive in terms of credit purpose or use of funds. Additionally, some banks active in this market are both extending equity bridge commitments and granting credit for dividend recapitalizations.

The amount of easing in commercial real estate (CRE) underwriting declined slightly. This is a positive change given that commercial real estate concentrations remain common.

	CRE—Commercial Construction			
	2004	2005	2006	2007
Eased	10%	29%	32%	28%
Unchanged	75%	63%	56%	59%
Tightened	15%	8%	12%	13%

	CRE—Residential Construction			
	2004	2005	2006	2007
Eased	5%	21%	25%	17%
Unchanged	85%	72%	64%	50%
Tightened	9%	7%	11%	33%

	CRE—All Other			
	2004	2005	2006	2007
Eased	8%	24%	32%	20%
Unchanged	83%	65%	60%	73%
Tightened	9%	11%	8%	7%

Methods of Easing

Examiners observed increasingly liberal repayment schemes and a marked decrease in the banks' ability to monitor credits via financial performance covenants. In addition to reduced loan fees and spreads, prominent methods of easing commercial underwriting standards include:

- relaxed loan structures,
- lower quality and lower financial strength of deals booked (i.e., both higher leverage and more sub-investment grade tranches),
- lengthened tenors,
- lower equity investment requirements,
- greater use of bond-like financial incurrence, rather than financial maintenance, covenants (i.e., covenant-lite structures), and
- liberal covenant thresholds (where maintenance covenants are used).

Nonbank investors generally have different expectations than commercial banks for deal structure, repayment terms, amount of acceptable leverage, and existence or type of loan covenants. Banks have originated large corporate and leveraged loans, often syndicated, to meet investor expectations and ensure market acceptance. These more accommodative standards are not new, but their use has become more widespread.

National banks purchasing any loans, including syndicated exposures, are obligated to perform their own credit analyses (including borrower repayment capacity) to make prudent credit decisions consistent with their own risk tolerance and management abilities.

As part of its 2007 underwriting survey, the OCC also assessed national bank credit exposures to hedge funds. Examiners reported that the principal source of credit exposure from hedge funds is counterparty credit risk from derivatives transactions, as hedge funds are not a material source of direct lending exposure. Examiners also noted that hedge funds continue to press banks for softer initial margin requirements. Initial margin is an additional source of collateral—beyond the collateral that secures current credit exposures—that protects a derivatives dealer against future changes in the value of derivatives contracts.

Retail Underwriting Standards

Examiners continue to note easing of retail credit standards; however, fewer surveyed banks eased standards than in the prior two years. Easing was most prevalent in large banks, where 65 percent of the banks eased standards. Tightening was noted mostly in community banks where 20 percent of the banks tightened standards. Examiners cited competition as the primary reason for this easing.

	All Banks—Retail Products			
	2004	2005	2006	2007
Eased	13%	28%	28%	20%
Unchanged	74%	62%	65%	67%
Tightened	13%	10%	7%	13%

Examiners reported current retail underwriting standards as predominately moderate in large banks (57 percent) and conservative in mid-size banks (62 percent), with community banks evenly divided between conservative and moderate. Examiners reached similar conclusions for residential real estate and home equity conventional loans, the dominant retail credit products in the surveyed banks.

Underwriting Standards	Banks		
	Large	Mid-Size	Community
Conservative	26%	62%	50%
Moderate	57%	31%	46%
Liberal	17%	7%	4%

Examiners concluded that retail credit risk increased in 29 percent of the banks over the prior 12 months, the highest percentage in the past five surveys. Further, examiners expect retail credit risk to increase in 36 percent of the banks in the next 12 months. Examiners cited rising interest rates, potential decreases in property values, and general economic conditions as factors contributing to the increased risk levels. Going forward, examiners expect that relaxed underwriting standards and product structures coupled with an uncertain economy will continue to increase the level of risk for the next 12 months.

Product Trends

At the product level, the easing that occurred in retail was most notable in home equity lending (conventional and high LTV) and residential real estate lending; however, the number of banks easing showed a decline in the 2007 survey. Examiners reported that 19 percent of the surveyed banks eased underwriting standards for residential mortgage lending, with similar easing in home equity. In addition, examiners noted an increased presence of nontraditional products such as interest-only loans and payment-option ARMs. In contrast to the 2006 survey when relatively few banks had tightened underwriting standards, examiners identified more banks tightening in the real estate areas in 2007, primarily in large banks. The tightening in home equity lending was attributed primarily to enhanced risk management, consistent with the home equity guidance detailed in OCC Bulletin 2005-22, "Home Equity Lending—Credit Risk Management Guidance."

	Home Equity—High LTV			
	2004	2005	2006	2007
Eased	18%	24%	37%	22%
Unchanged	71%	56%	63%	61%
Tightened	11%	20%	0%	17%

	Home Equity—Conventional			
	2004	2005	2006	2007
Eased	13%	27%	34%	19%
Unchanged	77%	62%	64%	65%
Tightened	10%	12%	2%	16%

	Residential Real Estate			
	2004	2005	2006	2007
Eased	7%	22%	26%	19%
Unchanged	86%	73%	69%	67%
Tightened	7%	5%	5%	14%

It is important to note that these product trends relate primarily to prime products as survey results reflect that few national banks offer subprime residential mortgages or subprime home equity lines or loans.

Product	# Banks Offering Product	# Banks with Subprime Product	Percent
Home Equity—High LTV	18	5	28%
Home Equity—Conventional	64	8	13%
Residential Real Estate	63	9	14%

There have been significant changes in market conditions and product performance since the survey was completed, especially as they relate to residential mortgage and home equity lending. As a result, many national banks have tightened underwriting standards for various residential real estate products and channels or discontinued some products all together.

Methods of Easing

Easing standards for home equity lending, both conventional and high LTV, include an increase of the maximum loan amount, lower credit score cutoffs, and higher allowable debt-to-income (DTI) and combined LTV ratios. Easing in residential real estate lending was centered in the expanded use of stated income, increased interest only periods, higher allowable LTV and DTI ratios, and protracted amortization periods. As noted above, many banks have responded to recent market changes with a general tightening of lending standards, including increased documentation and credit score requirements, and lower LTV constraints and qualifying debt ratios.

Eased standards have resulted in increased risk. Home equity lending, again, led the retail products exhibiting higher risk levels. For the 23 percent of surveyed banks reporting high LTV home equity lending, examiners noted increased risk in 55 percent of the banks over the prior year, and are forecasting increased risk in 72 percent of the banks over the next 12 months. For banks offering conventional home equity lending, examiners noted increased risk in 37 percent of the banks over the prior year, and anticipate increased risk in 45 percent of the banks over the next 12 months. None of the examiners reported decreasing risk for conventional home equity products in the past year.

Part II: Graphs and Tables

Commercial Credit Underwriting Trend

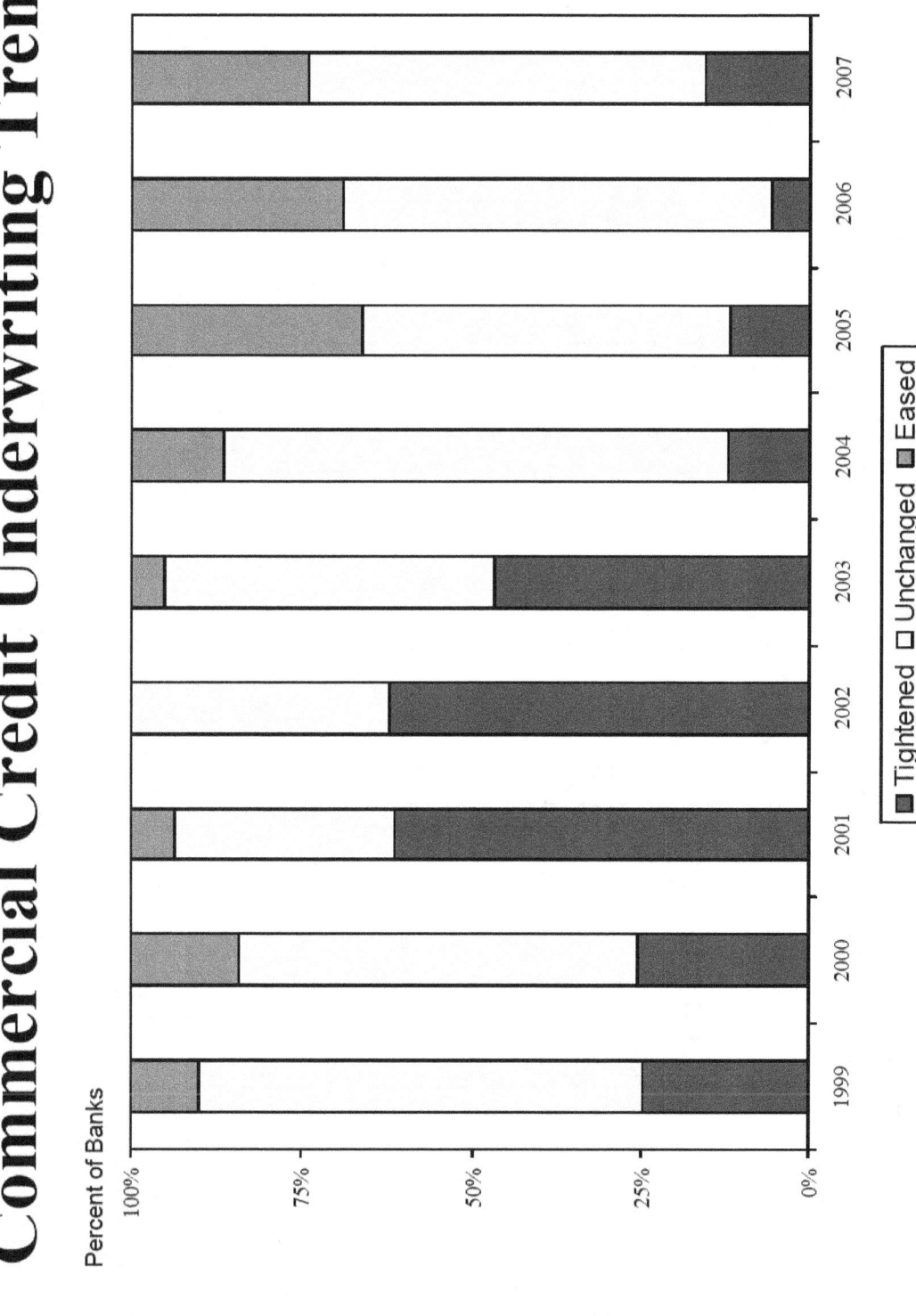

Percent of Banks

Tightened ☐ Unchanged ☐ Eased

1999 2000 2001 2002 2003 2004 2005 2006 2007

100% 75% 50% 25% 0%

Survey of Credit Underwriting: 2007

9

Commercial Underwriting Trends

By Product Type

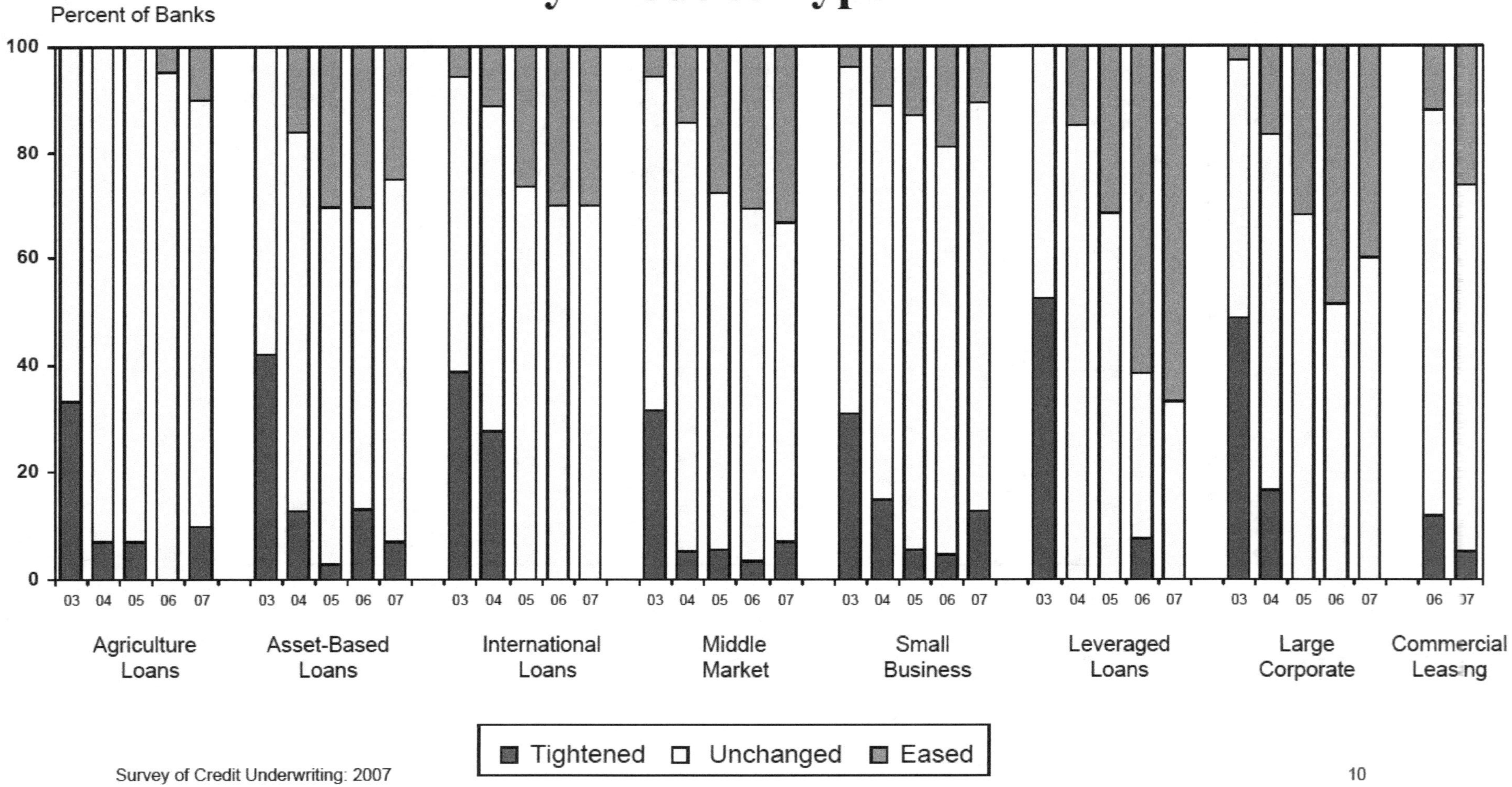

Percent of Banks
100
80
60
40
20
0
03 04 05 06 07
03 04 05 06 07
03 04 05 06 07
03 04 05 06 07
03 04 05 06 07
03 04 05 06 07
03 04 05 06 07
06 07
Agriculture Loans
Asset-Based Loans
International Loans
Middle Market
Small Business
Leveraged Loans
Large Corporate
Commercial Leasing
Tightened
Unchanged
Eased

Commercial Underwriting Trends

By Product Type

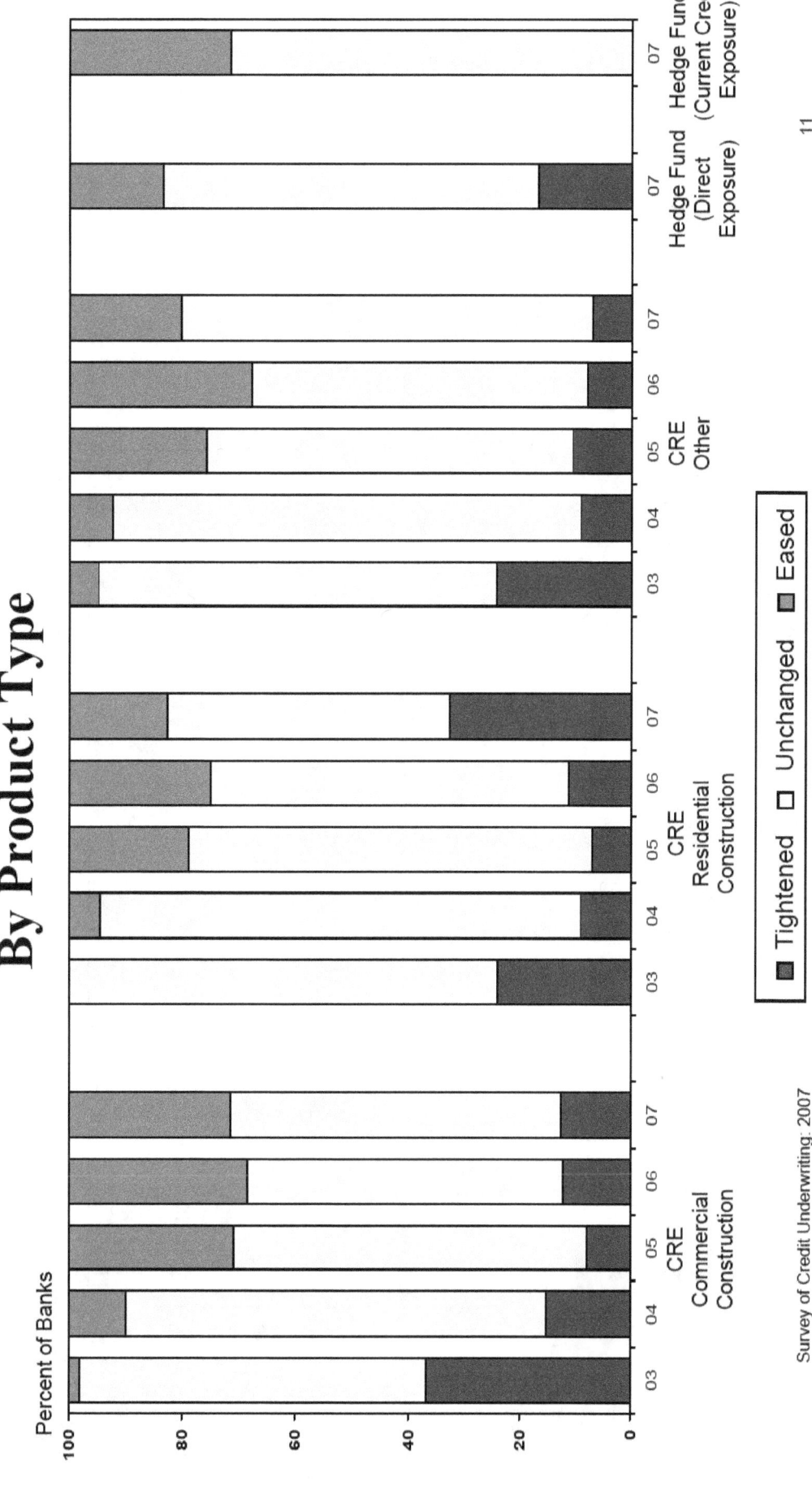

Survey of Credit Underwriting: 2007

11

Reasons for Changing Commercial Underwriting Standards

Percent of Banks

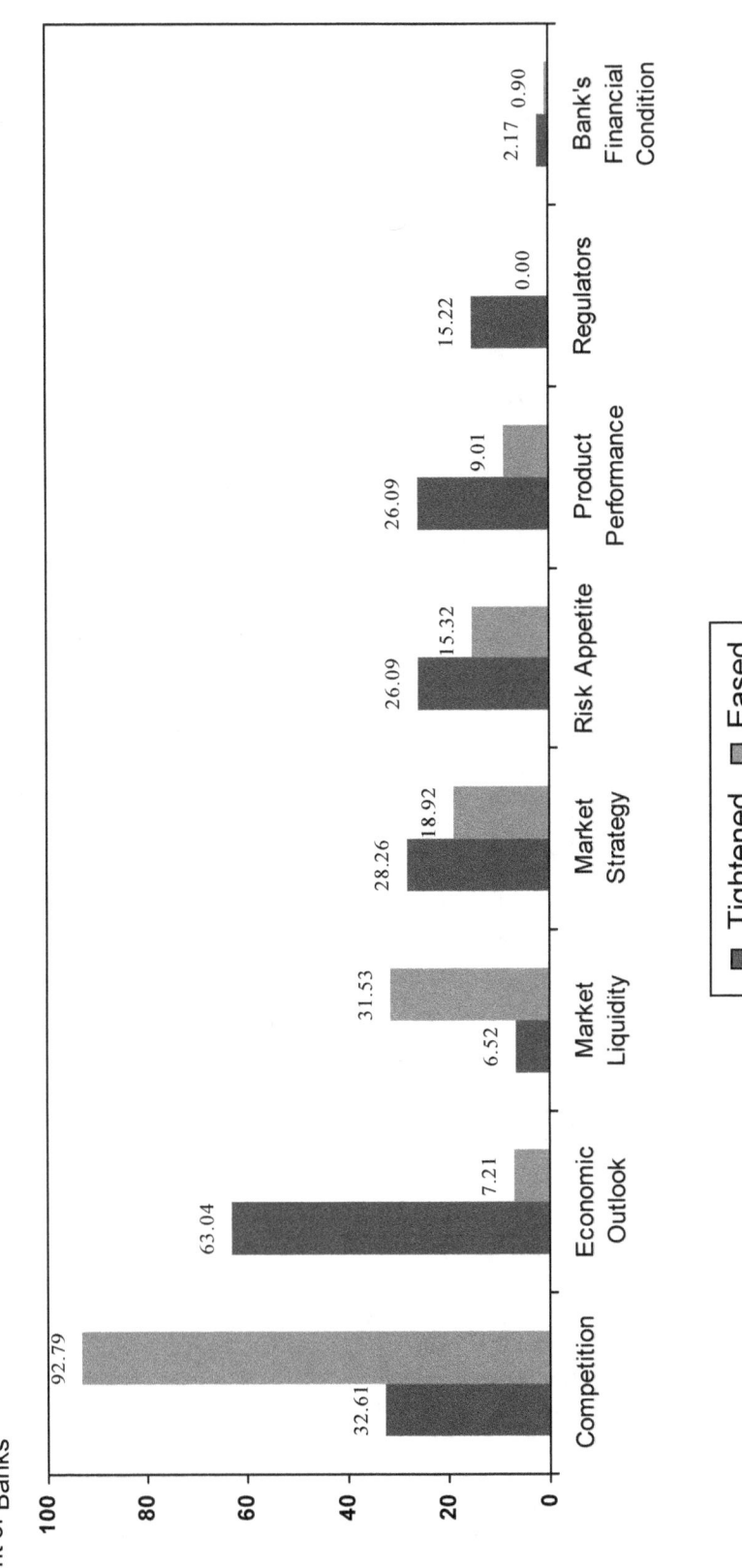

	Tightened	Eased
Competition	32.61	92.79
Economic Outlook	63.04	7.21
Market Liquidity	6.52	31.53
Market Strategy	28.26	18.92
Risk Appetite	26.09	15.32
Product Performance	26.09	9.01
Regulators	15.22	0.00
Bank's Financial Condition	2.17	0.90

■ Tightened ■ Eased

Survey of Credit Underwriting: 2007

Methods Used to Change
Commercial Underwriting Standards

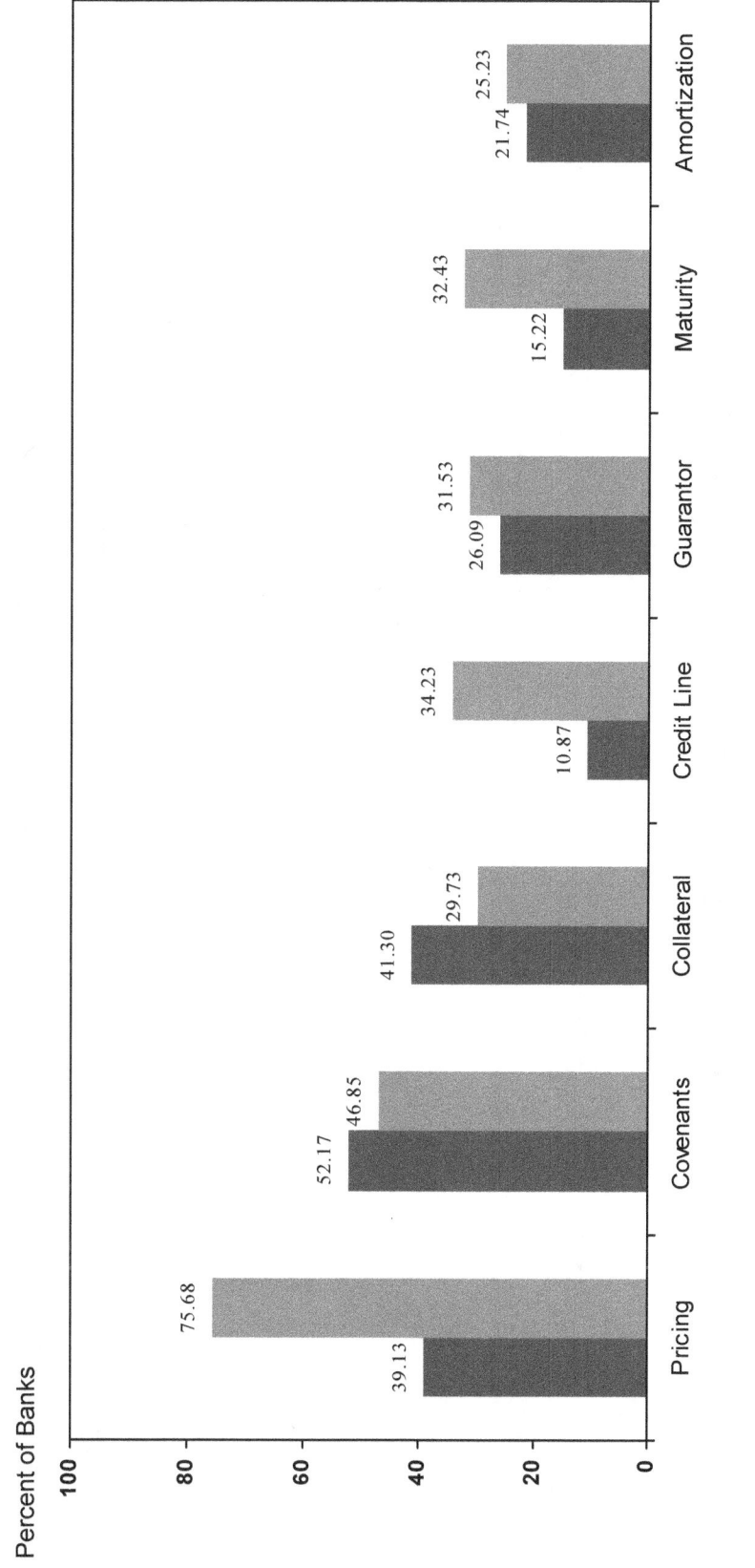

Percent of Banks

Legend: ■ Tightened ■ Eased

Method	Tightened	Eased
Pricing	39.13	75.68
Covenants	52.17	46.85
Collateral	41.30	29.73
Credit Line	10.87	34.23
Guarantor	26.09	31.53
Maturity	15.22	32.43
Amortization	21.74	25.23

Survey of Credit Underwriting: 2007

13

Commercial Credit Risk Trends

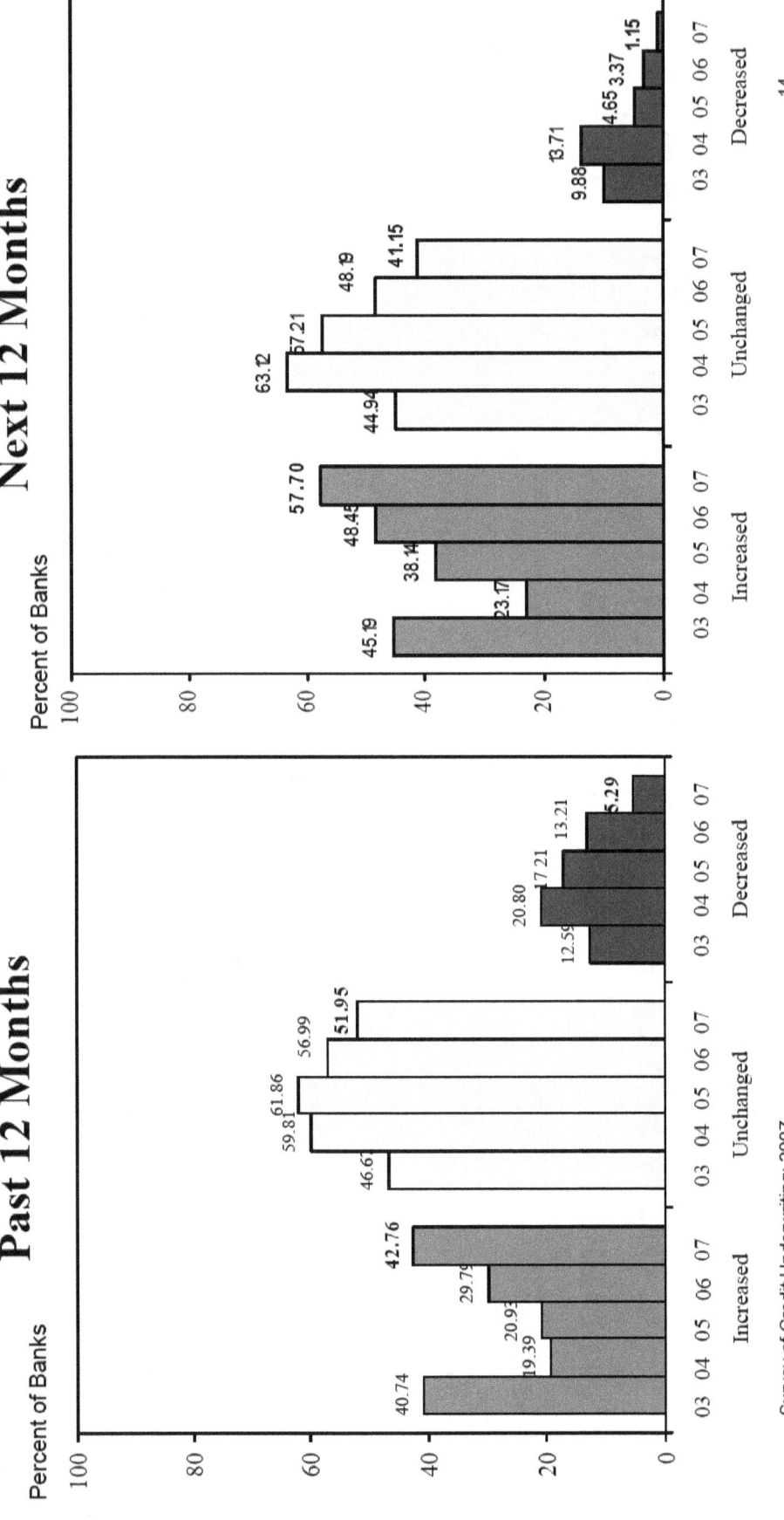

Past 12 Months

Percent of Banks

Increased: 40.74, 19.39, 20.93, 29.79, 42.76

Unchanged: 46.6, 59.81, 61.86, 56.99, 51.95

Decreased: 12.59, 20.80, 17.21, 13.21, 5.29

03 04 05 06 07 — Increased
03 04 05 06 07 — Unchanged
03 04 05 06 07 — Decreased

Next 12 Months

Percent of Banks

Increased: 45.19, 23.17, 38.14, 48.45, 57.70

Unchanged: 44.94, 63.12, 57.21, 48.19, 41.15

Decreased: 9.88, 13.71, 4.65, 3.37, 1.15

03 04 05 06 07 — Increased
03 04 05 06 07 — Unchanged
03 04 05 06 07 — Decreased

14

Survey of Credit Underwriting: 2007

Commercial Credit Risk Trends

Current Credit Risk Change By Product Type

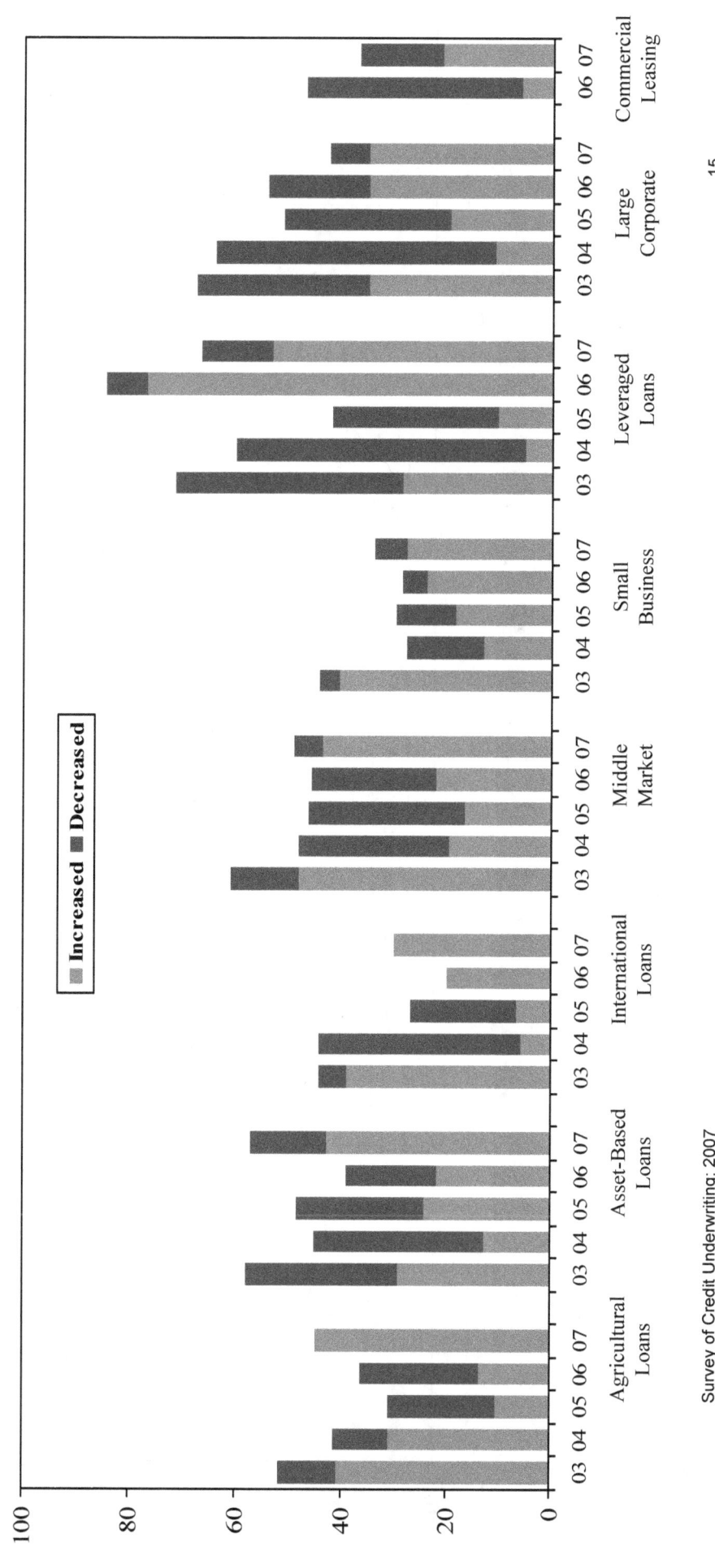

Survey of Credit Underwriting: 2007

15

Commercial Credit Risk Trends

Current Credit Risk Change By Product Type

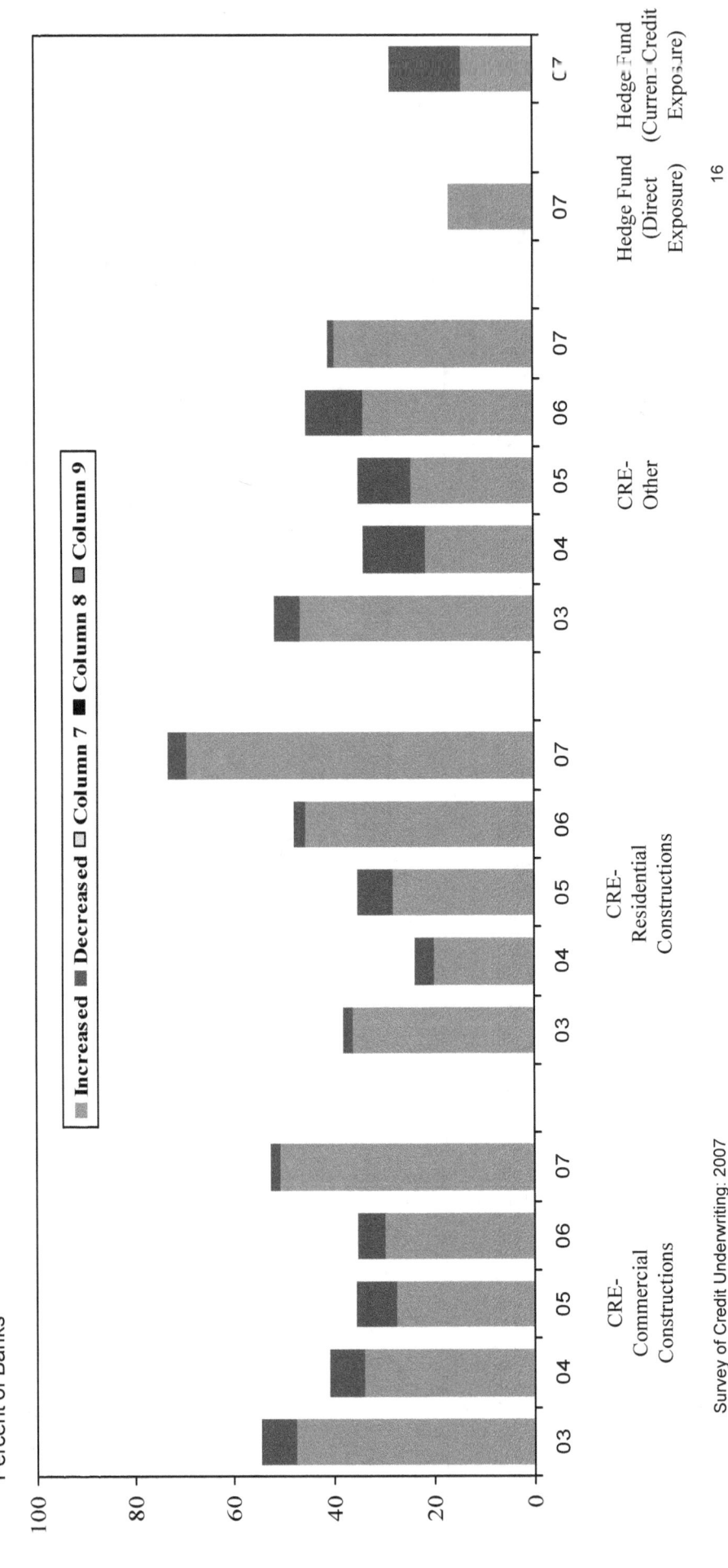

Percent of Banks

Survey of Credit Underwriting: 2007

16

Retail Credit Underwriting Trend

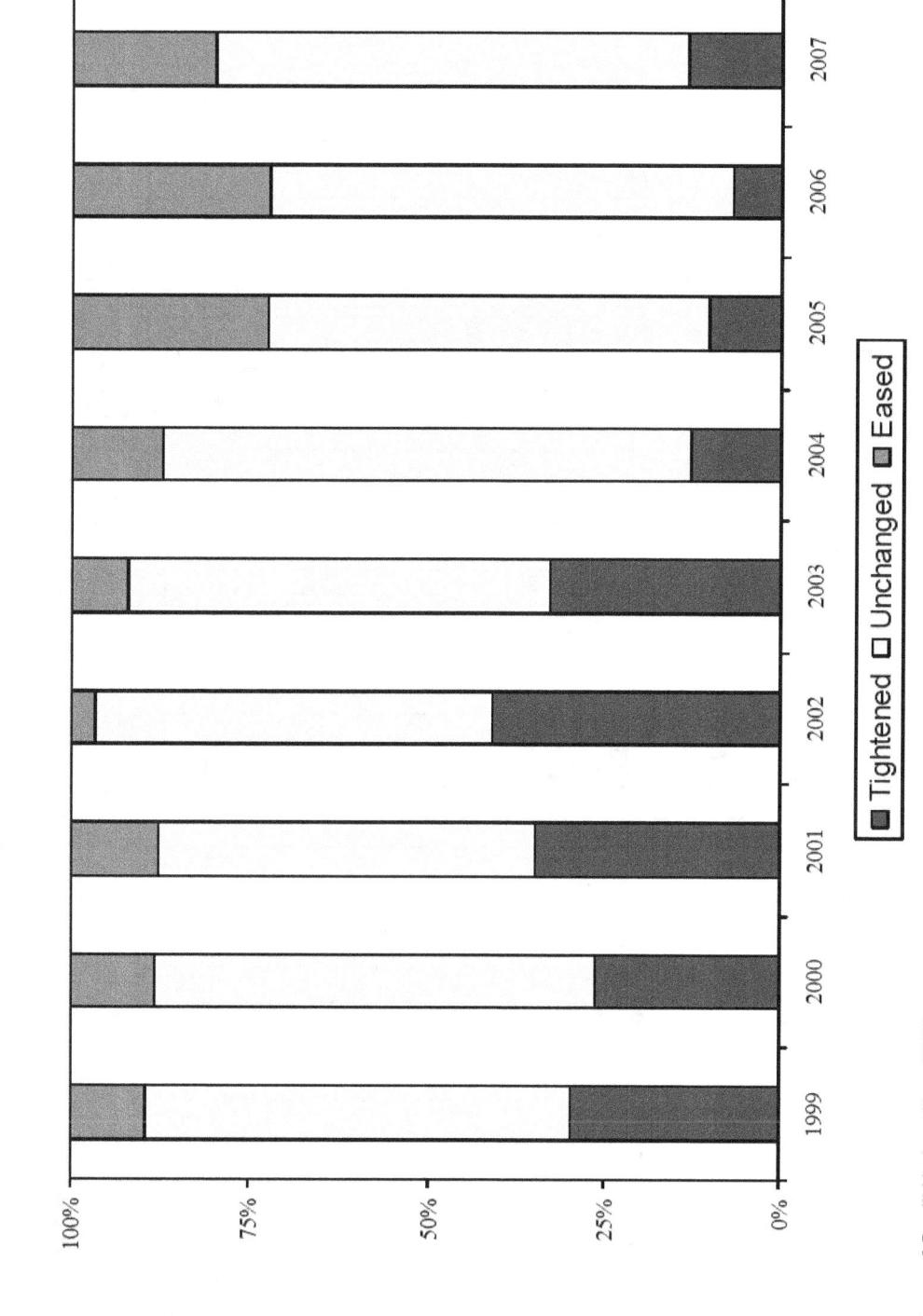

Survey of Credit Underwriting: 2007

Retail Underwriting Trends

By Product Type

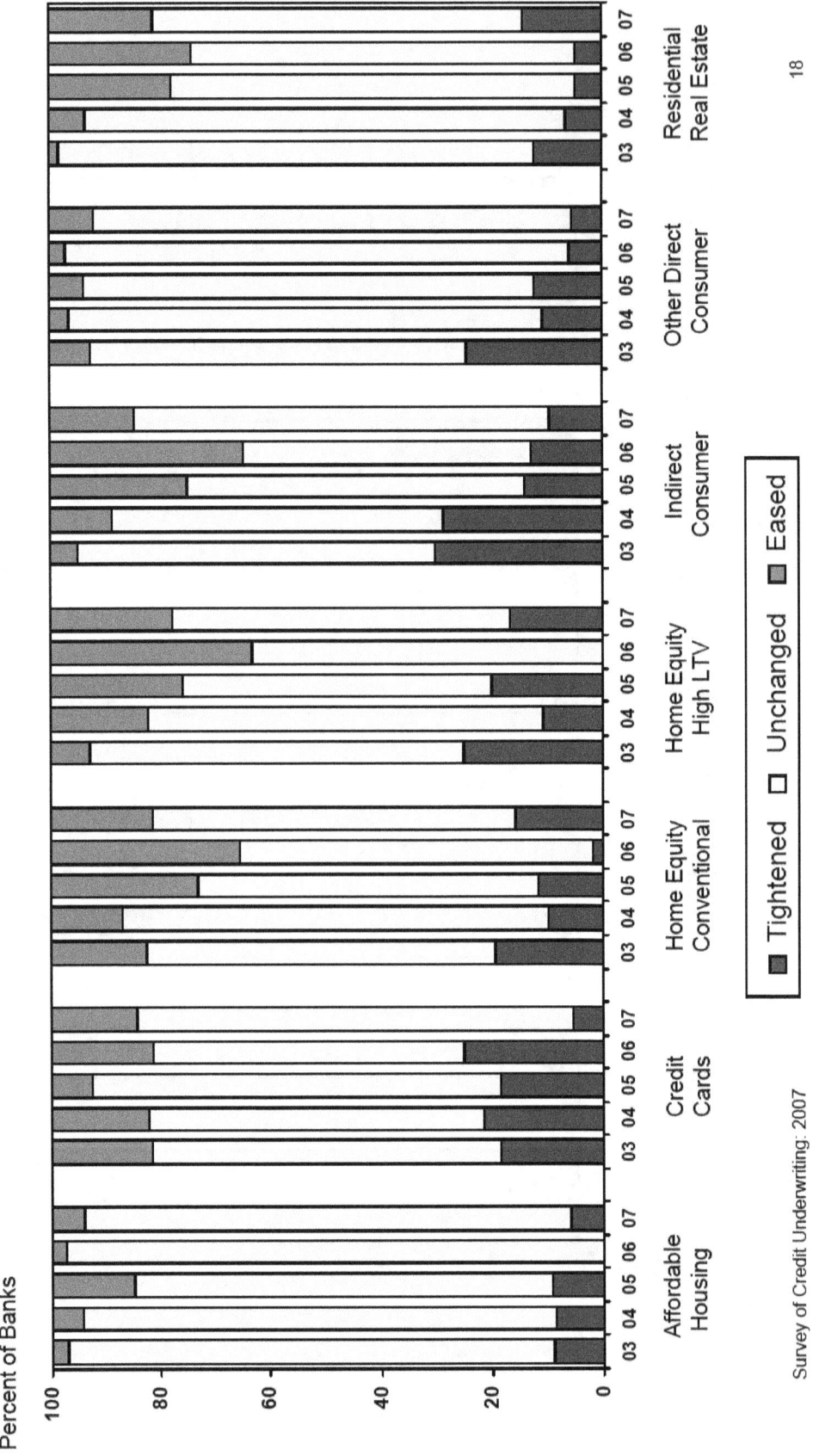

Percent of Banks

Legend: ■ Tightened □ Unchanged ■ Eased

Affordable Housing — 03 04 05 06 07
Credit Cards — 03 04 05 06 07
Home Equity Conventional — 03 04 05 06 07
Home Equity High LTV — 03 04 05 06 07
Indirect Consumer — 03 04 05 06 07
Other Direct Consumer — 03 04 05 06 07
Residential Real Estate — 03 04 05 06 07

Reasons for Changing
Retail Underwriting Standards

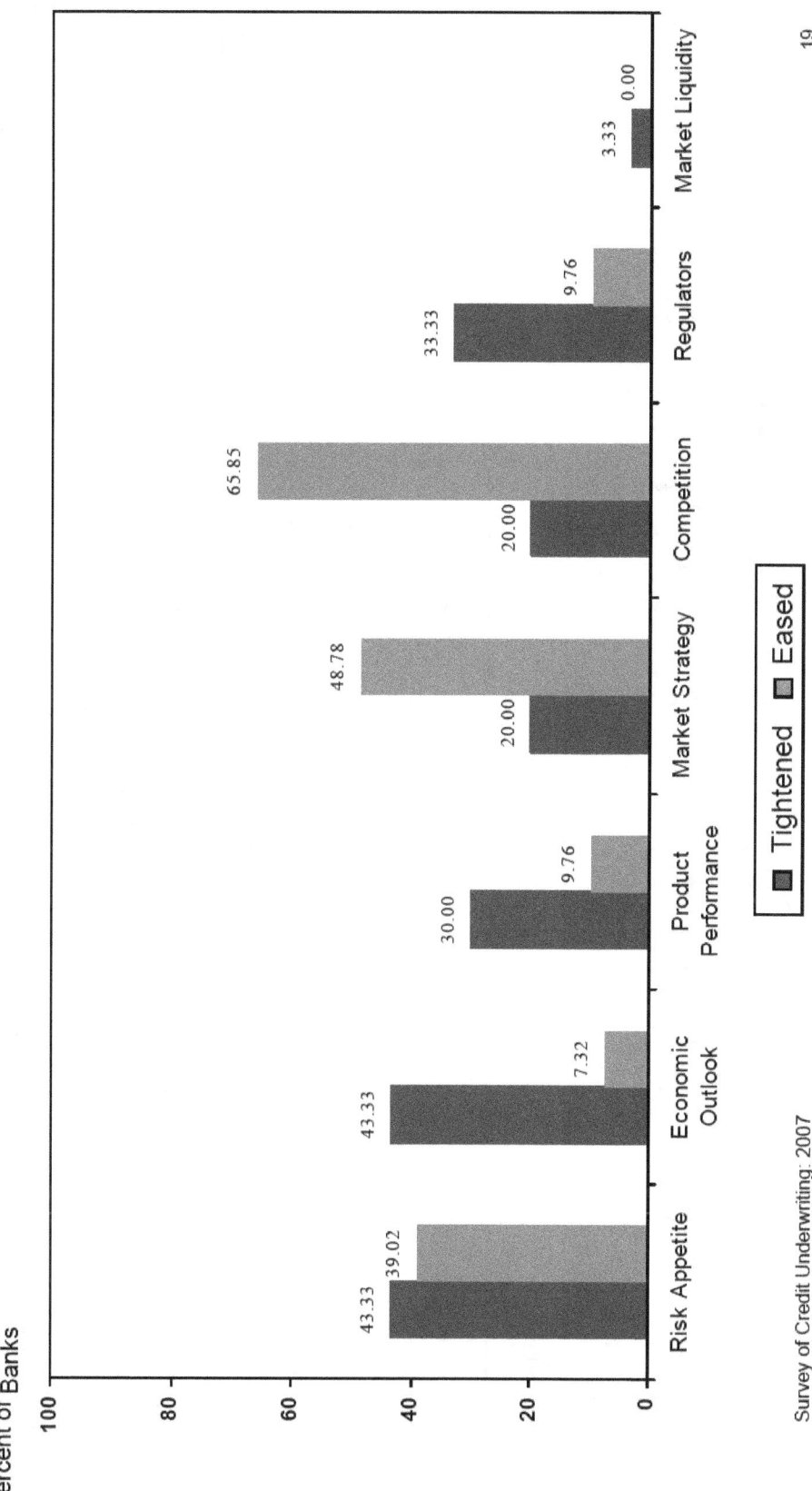

Percent of Banks

Survey of Credit Underwriting: 2007

19

Methods Used to Change
Retail Underwriting Standards

Percent of Banks

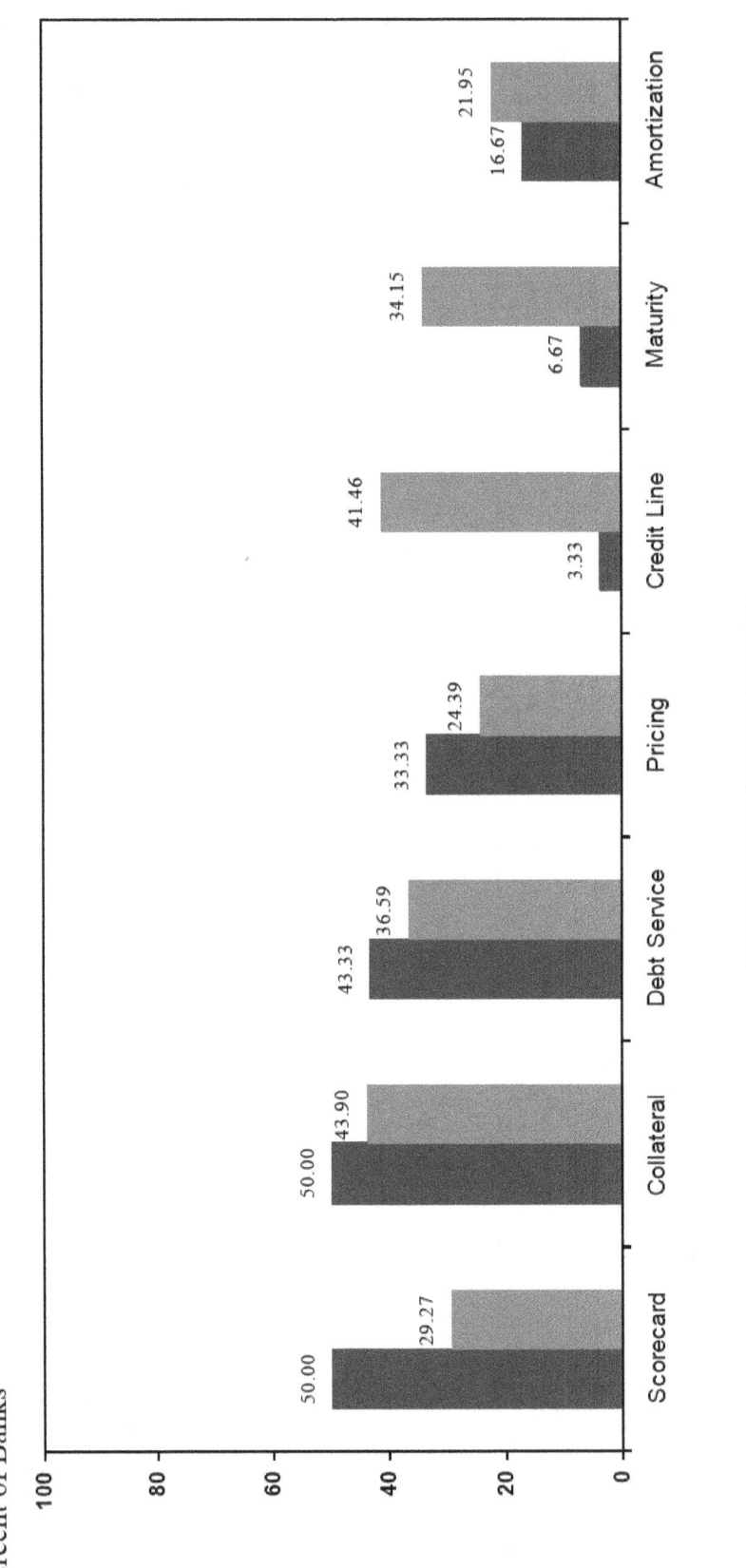

Survey of Credit Underwriting: 2007

Retail Credit Risk Trends

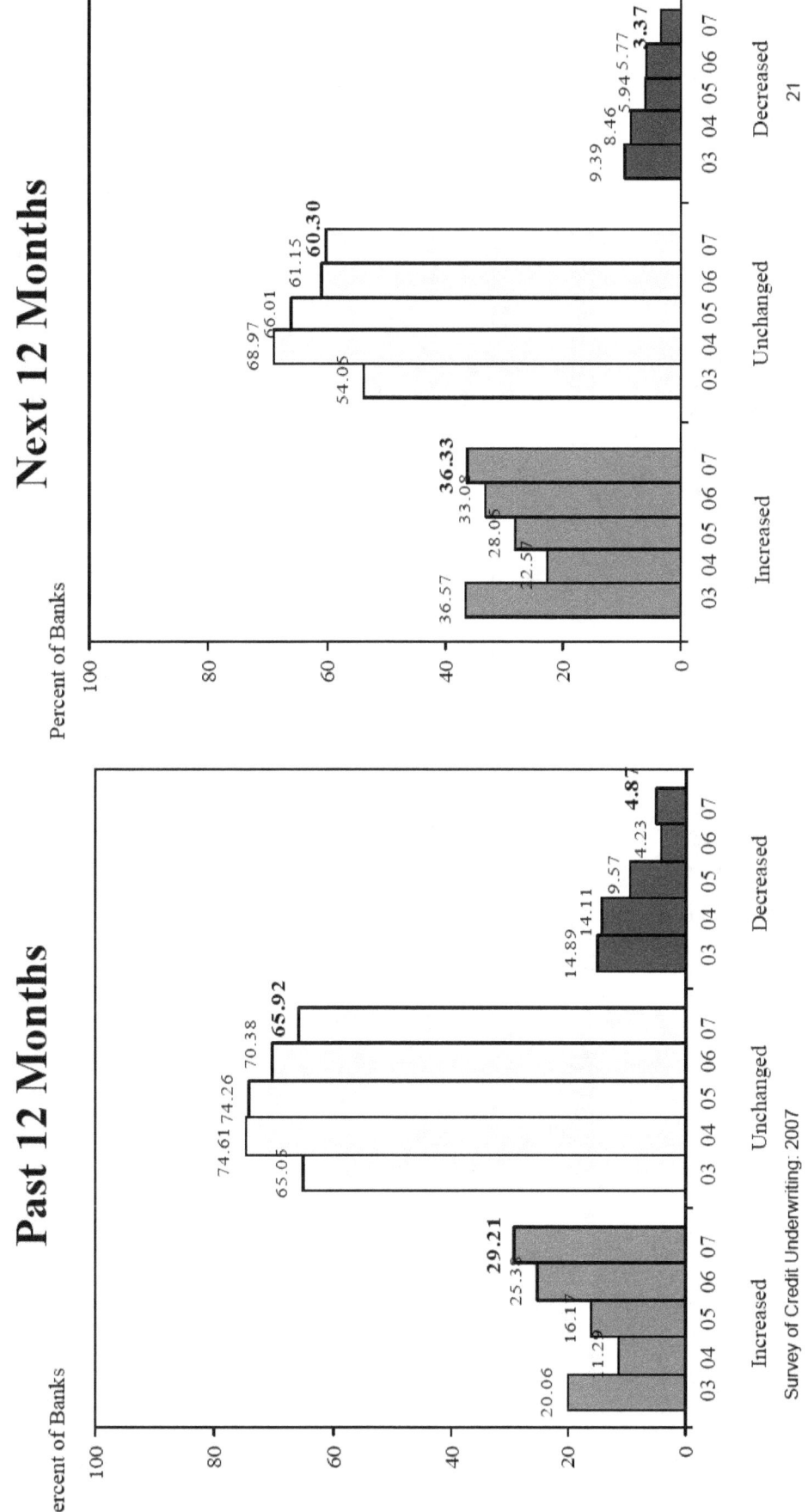

Past 12 Months

Percent of Banks

Survey of Credit Underwriting: 2007

Next 12 Months

Percent of Banks

Retail Credit Risk Trends

Current Credit Risk Change By Product Type

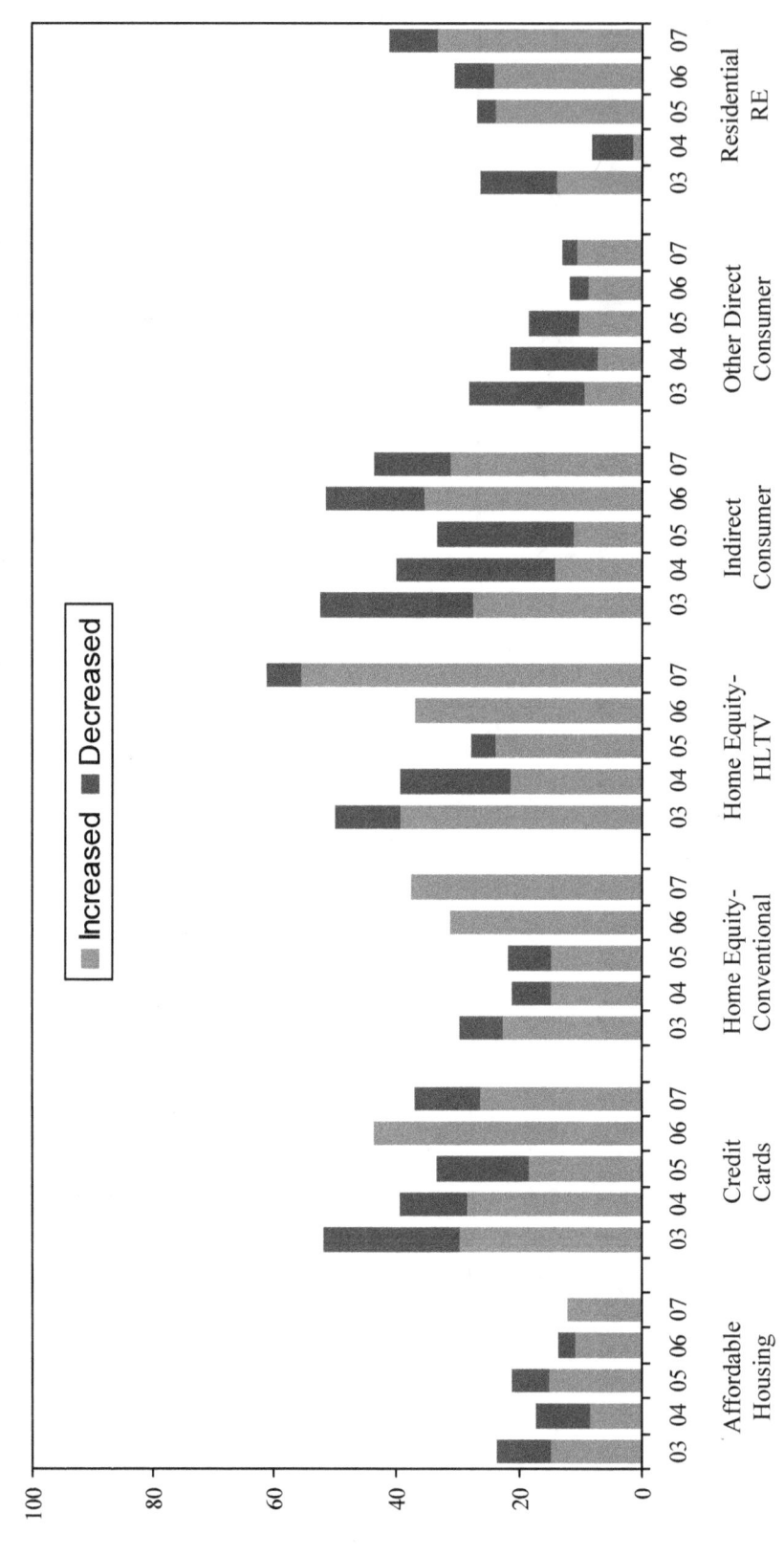

Percent of Banks

Survey of Credit Underwriting: 2007

22

Tables: Commercial Lending Portfolios

Agricultural Lending

Twenty of the 78 banks in the survey were engaged in some form of agricultural lending.

Changes in Underwriting Standards in Agricultural Loan Portfolios
(Percent of Banks)

	Eased	Unchanged	Tightened
1999	3	79	18
2000	3	71	26
2001	3	71	26
2002	0	70	30
2003	0	67	33
2004	0	93	7
2005	0	93	7
2006	5	95	0
2007	10	80	10

Changes in the Level of Credit Risk in Agricultural Loan Portfolios
(Percent of Banks)

	Declined Significantly	Declined Somewhat	Unchanged	Increased Somewhat	Increased Significantly
1999	0	6	42	49	3
2000	0	15	41	44	0
2001	0	17	43	34	6
2002	0	7	63	30	0
2003	0	11	48	41	0
2004	0	10	59	31	0
2005	4	17	69	10	0
2006	0	23	63	14	0
2007	0	0	55	45	0
Future 12 Months	0	0	60	40	0

Asset-Based Loans

Twenty-eight banks in the survey were engaged in asset-based lending.

Changes in Underwriting Standards in Asset-Based Loan Portfolios
(Percent of Banks)

	Eased	Unchanged	Tightened
1999	10	78	12
2000	11	67	22
2001	5	53	42
2002	3	66	31
2003	0	58	42
2004	16	71	13
2005	30	67	3
2006	30	57	13
2007	25	68	7

Changes in the Level of Credit Risk in Asset-Based Loan Portfolios
(Percent of Banks)

	Declined Significantly	Declined Somewhat	Unchanged	Increased Somewhat	Increased Significantly
1999	0	10	66	24	0
2000	0	8	62	30	0
2001	5	8	42	45	0
2002	0	0	50	50	0
2003	3	26	42	29	0
2004	3	29	55	13	0
2005	0	24	52	24	0
2006	0	17	61	22	0
2007	0	14	43	43	0
Future 12 Months	0	0	54	46	0

Commercial Leasing

Commercial leasing was offered by 19 of the banks in the survey.

Changes in Underwriting Standards in Commercial Leasing Portfolios
(Percent of Banks)

	Eased	Unchanged	Tightened
2006	12	76	12
2007	26	69	5

Changes in the Level of Credit Risk in Commercial Leasing Portfolios
(Percent of Banks)

	Declined Significantly	Declined Somewhat	Unchanged	Increased Somewhat	Increased Significantly
2006	6	35	53	6	0
2007	0	16	63	21	0
Future 12 Months	0	10	53	37	0

Commercial Real Estate Lending — Commercial Construction

Sixty-three of the banks in the survey were engaged in commercial construction lending.

Changes in Underwriting Standards in Commercial Construction Loan Portfolios
(Percent of Banks)

	Eased	Unchanged	Tightened
2003	2	61	37
2004	10	75	15
2005	29	63	8
2006	32	56	12
2007	28	59	13

Changes in the Level of Credit Risk in Commercial Construction Loan Portfolios
(Percent of Banks)

	Declined Significantly	Declined Somewhat	Unchanged	Increased Somewhat	Increased Significantly
2003	0	7	46	42	5
2004	0	7	59	34	0
2005	2	5	65	28	0
2006	0	5	65	30	0
2007	0	2	48	49	1
Future 12 Months	0	2	33	62	3

Commercial Real Estate Lending — Residential Construction

Fifty-two of the banks in the survey were engaged in residential construction lending.

Changes in Underwriting Standards in Residential Construction Loan Portfolios
(Percent of Banks)

	Eased	Unchanged	Tightened
2003	0	76	24
2004	5	86	9
2005	21	72	7
2006	25	64	11
2007	17	50	33

Changes in the Level of Credit Risk in Residential Construction Loan Portfolios
(Percent of Banks)

	Declined Significantly	Declined Somewhat	Unchanged	Increased Somewhat	Increased Significantly
2003	0	2	62	34	2
2004	0	4	76	18	2
2005	2	6	65	27	0
2006	0	2	52	46	0
2007	0	4	27	63	6
Future 12 Months	0	2	29	67	2

Commercial Real Estate Lending — Other

Seventy-one of the banks in the survey were engaged in other commercial real estate lending.

Changes in Underwriting Standards in Other Commercial Real Estate Loan Portfolios
(Percent of Banks)

	Eased	Unchanged	Tightened
2003	5	71	24
2004	8	83	9
2005	24	65	11
2006	32	60	8
2007	20	73	7

Changes in the Level of Credit Risk in Other Commercial Real Estate Loan Portfolios
(Percent of Banks)

	Declined Significantly	Declined Somewhat	Unchanged	Increased Somewhat	Increased Significantly
2003	0	5	48	43	4
2004	0	12	66	20	2
2005	2	9	65	24	0
2006	1	10	55	34	0
2007	0	2	59	38	1
Future 12 Months	0	0	45	52	3

International Lending

Only 10 of the banks in the survey were active in international lending.

Changes in Underwriting Standards in International Loan Portfolios
(Percent of Banks)

	Eased	Unchanged	Tightened
1999	4	54	42
2000	14	72	14
2001	29	57	14
2002	11	61	28
2003	6	55	39
2004	11	61	28
2005	27	73	0
2006	30	70	0
2007	30	70	0

Changes in the Level of Credit Risk in International Loan Portfolios
(Percent of Banks)

	Declined Significantly	Declined Somewhat	Unchanged	Increased Somewhat	Increased Significantly
1999	8	8	42	38	4
2000	0	33	53	14	0
2001	0	14	53	33	0
2002	0	22	39	28	11
2003	0	6	55	33	6
2004	6	33	55	6	0
2005	0	20	73	7	0
2006	0	0	80	20	0
2007	0	0	70	30	0
Future 12 Months	0	0	60	40	0

Middle Market Lending

Fifty-seven of the banks in the survey were engaged in middle market lending.

Changes in Underwriting Standards in Middle Market Loan Portfolios
(Percent of Banks)

	Eased	Unchanged	Tightened
1999	18	73	9
2000	18	66	16
2001	11	48	41
2002	0	60	40
2003	6	63	31
2004	14	81	5
2005	28	67	5
2006	31	66	3
2007	33	60	7

Changes in the Level of Credit Risk in Middle Market Loan Portfolios
(Percent of Banks)

	Declined Significantly	Declined Somewhat	Unchanged	Increased Somewhat	Increased Significantly
1999	0	8	56	36	0
2000	0	2	50	46	2
2001	0	2	35	59	4
2002	2	8	22	66	2
2003	0	13	39	44	4
2004	0	28	52	18	2
2005	4	26	54	16	0
2006	0	24	54	20	2
2007	0	5	51	44	0
Future 12 Months	0	0	44	56	0

Small Business Lending

Forty-seven of the banks in the survey were lending in the small business market.

Changes in Underwriting Standards in Small Business Loan Portfolios
(Percent of Banks)

	Eased	Unchanged	Tightened
1999	13	75	12
2000	8	73	19
2001	5	63	32
2002	2	66	32
2003	4	65	31
2004	11	74	15
2005	13	81	6
2006	19	76	5
2007	11	76	13

Changes in the Level of Credit Risk in Small Business Loan Portfolios
(Percent of Banks)

	Declined Significantly	Declined Somewhat	Unchanged	Increased Somewhat	Increased Significantly
1999	0	8	67	23	2
2000	0	3	72	22	3
2001	0	3	60	37	0
2002	0	2	56	40	2
2003	0	4	56	38	2
2004	0	15	72	13	0
2005	0	11	70	19	0
2006	0	5	71	22	2
2007	2	4	66	26	2
Future 12 Months	0	0	43	55	2

Leveraged Loans

Fifteen of the banks in the survey provided leveraged loans.

Changes in Underwriting Standards in Leveraged Loan Portfolios
(Percent of Banks)

	Eased	Unchanged	Tightened
1999	24	44	32
2000	35	45	20
2001	0	4	96
2002	0	44	56
2003	0	48	52
2004	15	85	0
2005	32	68	0
2006	61	31	8
2007	67	33	0

Changes in the Level of Credit Risk in Leveraged Loan Portfolios
(Percent of Banks)

	Declined Significantly	Declined Somewhat	Unchanged	Increased Somewhat	Increased Significantly
1999	0	4	36	56	4
2000	0	0	20	80	0
2001	0	4	8	46	42
2002	0	7	26	52	15
2003	10	33	28	29	0
2004	15	40	40	5	0
2005	5	27	58	5	5
2006	0	8	15	69	8
2007	0	13	34	53	0
Future 12 Months	0	0	20	80	0

Large Corporate Loans

Forty of the banks in the survey were active in large corporate loan market.

Changes in Underwriting Standards in Large Corporate Loan Portfolios
(Percent of Banks)

	Eased	Unchanged	Tightened
1999	18	50	32
2000	22	61	17
2001	0	34	66
2002	0	45	55
2003	3	49	48
2004	17	66	17
2005	32	68	0
2006	49	51	0
2007	40	60	0

Changes in the Level of Credit Risk in Large Corporate Loan Portfolios
(Percent of Banks)

	Declined Significantly	Declined Somewhat	Unchanged	Increased Somewhat	Increased Significantly
1999	0	0	45	45	10
2000	0	0	36	61	3
2001	0	6	17	63	14
2002	0	8	29	53	10
2003	5	27	33	30	5
2004	17	36	36	11	0
2005	5	27	49	19	0
2006	0	19	46	32	3
2007	0	8	57	35	0
Future 12 Months	0	3	35	62	0

Hedge Funds (Direct Credit Exposure)

Only six of the banks in the survey were active in direct lending to hedge funds.

Changes in Underwriting Standards in Hedge Funds (Direct Credit Exposure)
(Percent of Banks)

	Eased	Unchanged	Tightened
2007	17	66	17

Changes in the Level of Credit Risk in Hedge Funds (Direct Credit Exposure)
(Percent of Banks)

	Declined Significantly	Declined Somewhat	Unchanged	Increased Somewhat	Increased Significantly
2007	0	0	83	17	0
Future 12 Months	0	0	67	33	0

Hedge Funds (Counterparty Credit Exposure)

Only seven of the banks in the survey had sizable counterparty credit exposures to hedge funds.

Changes in Underwriting Standards in Hedge Funds (Counterparty Credit Exposure)
(Percent of Banks)

	Eased	Unchanged	Tightened
2007	29	71	0

Changes in the Level of Credit Risk in Hedge Funds (Counterparty Credit Exposure)
(Percent of Banks)

	Declined Significantly	Declined Somewhat	Unchanged	Increased Somewhat	Increased Significantly
2007	0	14	72	14	0
Future 12 Months	0	0	29	71	0

Tables: Retail Lending Portfolios

Affordable Housing Lending

Thirty-three of the banks in the survey were reported to have made affordable housing loans.

Changes in Underwriting Standards in Affordable Housing Loan Portfolios
(Percent of Banks)

	Eased	Unchanged	Tightened
1999	16	70	14
2000	10	84	6
2001	6	88	6
2002	3	91	6
2003	3	88	9
2004	6	86	8
2005	15	76	9
2006	3	97	0
2007	6	88	6

Changes in the Level of Credit Risk in Affordable Housing Loan Portfolios
(Percent of Banks)

	Declined Significantly	Declined Somewhat	Unchanged	Increased Somewhat	Increased Significantly
1999	2	2	78	18	0
2000	0	6	83	11	0
2001	2	2	88	8	0
2002	0	6	73	21	0
2003	0	9	76	15	0
2004	0	9	82	9	0
2005	0	6	79	15	0
2006	0	3	86	11	0
2007	0	0	88	12	0
Future 12 Months	0	3	70	27	0

Affordable housing loans include all types of loans on affordable housing for low- and moderate-income individuals and families, including single- to four-family and multifamily dwellings.

Credit Card Lending

Nineteen of the banks in the survey banks were engaged in credit card lending.

Changes in Underwriting Standards in Credit Card Loan Portfolios
(Percent of Banks)

	Eased	Unchanged	Tightened
1999	8	66	26
2000	9	75	16
2001	16	60	24
2002	12	66	22
2003	19	62	19
2004	18	61	21
2005	7	74	19
2006	19	56	25
2007	16	79	5

Changes in the Level of Credit Risk in Credit Card Loan Portfolios
(Percent of Banks)

	Declined Significantly	Declined Somewhat	Unchanged	Increased Somewhat	Increased Significantly
1999	0	13	47	36	4
2000	0	16	66	16	2
2001	8	5	57	27	3
2002	0	6	54	31	9
2003	0	22	48	30	0
2004	0	11	61	25	3
2005	0	15	67	18	0
2006	0	0	56	44	0
2007	0	11	63	26	0
Future 12 Months	0	0	74	26	0

Direct Consumer Lending

Thirty-eight of the banks in the survey were engaged in direct consumer lending.

Changes in Underwriting Standards in Other Direct Consumer Loan Portfolios
(Percent of Banks)

	Eased	Unchanged	Tightened
1999	7	74	19
2000	10	78	12
2001	7	73	20
2002	2	67	31
2003	8	68	24
2004	3	86	11
2005	6	82	12
2006	3	91	6
2007	8	87	5

Changes in the Level of Credit Risk in Other Direct Consumer Loan Portfolios
(Percent of Banks)

	Declined Significantly	Declined Somewhat	Unchanged	Increased Somewhat	Increased Significantly
1999	0	7	65	28	0
2000	0	9	74	15	2
2001	0	7	71	20	2
2002	2	6	67	25	0
2003	2	17	72	7	2
2004	2	13	78	7	0
2005	0	8	82	10	0
2006	0	3	88	9	0
2007	0	3	87	10	0
Future 12 Months	0	3	84	13	0

Home Equity — Conventional Lending

Sixty-four of the banks in the survey offered the conventional home equity lending product.

Changes in Underwriting Standards in Home Equity — Conventional Loan Portfolios
(Percent of Banks)

	Eased	Unchanged	Tightened
1999	23	67	10
2000	23	64	13
2001	7	70	23
2002	0	74	26
2003	18	63	19
2004	13	77	10
2005	27	62	11
2006	34	64	2
2007	19	65	16

Changes in the Level of Credit Risk in Home Equity — Conventional Loan Portfolios
(Percent of Banks)

	Declined Significantly	Declined Somewhat	Unchanged	Increased Somewhat	Increased Significantly
1999	0	0	69	29	2
2000	0	5	73	20	2
2001	0	11	74	13	2
2002	0	7	71	22	0
2003	4	4	69	23	0
2004	0	6	79	13	2
2005	0	7	78	15	0
2006	0	0	69	29	2
2007	0	0	63	34	3
Future 12 Months	0	0	55	44	1

Home Equity — High LTV Lending

Eighteen of the banks in the survey offered the high LTV home equity lending product.

Changes in Underwriting Standards in Home Equity — High LTV Loan Portfolios
(Percent of Banks)

	Eased	Unchanged	Tightened
1999	20	61	19
2000	21	55	24
2001	11	54	35
2002	0	56	44
2003	7	68	25
2004	18	71	11
2005	24	56	20
2006	37	63	0
2007	22	61	17

Changes in the Level of Credit Risk in Home Equity — High LTV Loan Portfolios
(Percent of Banks)

	Declined Significantly	Declined Somewhat	Unchanged	Increased Somewhat	Increased Significantly
1999	0	6	47	44	3
2000	0	13	58	24	5
2001	5	11	62	16	6
2002	0	12	40	44	4
2003	0	11	50	36	3
2004	0	18	61	18	3
2005	0	4	72	24	0
2006	0	0	63	37	0
2007	0	6	39	55	0
Future 12 Months	0	0	28	72	0

Indirect Consumer Lending

Thirty-two of the banks in the survey were engaged in indirect consumer lending.

Changes in Underwriting Standards in Indirect Consumer Loan Portfolios
(Percent of Banks)

	Eased	Unchanged	Tightened
1999	7	56	37
2000	7	60	33
2001	7	63	30
2002	0	72	28
2003	5	65	30
2004	11	60	29
2005	25	61	14
2006	35	52	13
2007	16	75	9

Changes in the Level of Credit Risk in Indirect Consumer Loan Portfolios
(Percent of Banks)

	Declined Significantly	Declined Somewhat	Unchanged	Increased Somewhat	Increased Significantly
1999	2	23	42	33	0
2000	7	16	55	22	0
2001	2	21	39	33	5
2002	3	13	38	43	3
2003	5	20	47	28	0
2004	0	26	60	14	0
2005	3	19	67	8	3
2006	6	10	48	36	0
2007	0	3	87	10	0
Future 12 Months	3	10	53	34	0

Residential Real Estate Lending

Sixty-three of the banks in the survey were engaged in residential real estate lending.

Changes in Underwriting Standards in Residential Real Estate Loan Portfolios
(Percent of Banks)

	Eased	Unchanged	Tightened
1999	14	77	9
2000	7	85	8
2001	12	72	16
2002	4	83	13
2003	2	86	12
2004	7	86	7
2005	22	73	5
2006	26	69	5
2007	19	67	14

Changes in the Level of Credit Risk in Residential Real Estate Loan Portfolios
(Percent of Banks)

	Declined Significantly	Declined Somewhat	Unchanged	Increased Somewhat	Increased Significantly
1999	3	5	71	21	0
2000	0	3	83	12	2
2001	0	9	76	15	0
2002	0	8	68	24	0
2003	0	12	74	12	2
2004	0	6	92	2	0
2005	0	3	73	24	0
2006	0	7	69	24	0
2007	2	6	59	33	0
Future 12 Months	2	3	55	40	0